U.S. PRESIDENTS

MYTHS OR FACTS?

MYTHS AND FACTS ABOUT THEODORE ROOSEVELT

EZRA E. KNOPP

PowerKiDS press

Published in 2024 by The Rosen Publishing Group, Inc.
2544 Clinton Street, Buffalo, NY 14224

First Edition

Editor: Greg Roza
Book Design: Michael Flynn

Photo Credits: Cover Werkat/Shutterstock.com; (series background) Azamatovic/Shutterstock.com; p. 5 (Theodore Sr.) https://commons.wikimedia.org/wiki/File:Portrait_of_Theodore_Roosevelt,_Sr._(e4ca9c8c-5023-4449-af2b-db44da700528).jpg; p. 5 (Theodore Jr.) https://commons.wikimedia.org/wiki/File:TR_Age_11_Paris.jpg; p. 7 https://commons.wikimedia.org/wiki/File:Lincoln_Funeral_Procession_Roosevelt_Mansion_Broadway.jpg; p. 8 https://en.wikipedia.org/wiki/File:Muir_and_Roosevelt_restored.jpg; p. 11 https://commons.wikimedia.org/wiki/File:Theodore_Roosevelt_Inaugural_National_Historic_Site_-_Oct_2022_-_52923257895.jpg; pp. 13, 17 Everett Collection/Shutterstock.com; p. 15 https://commons.wikimedia.org/wiki/File:WCMorris_Spokesman-Review_cartoons_099_(1).jpg; p. 19 courtesy of the Library of Congress.

Library of Congress Cataloging-in-Publication Data

Names: Knopp, Ezra E., author.
Title: Myths and facts about Theodore Roosevelt / Ezra E. Knopp.
Description: Buffalo : PowerKids Press, [2024] | Series: U.S. presidents: myths of facts? | Includes bibliographical references and index.
Identifiers: LCCN 2023036954 (print) | LCCN 2023036955 (ebook) | ISBN 9781499444148 (library binding) | ISBN 9781499444131 (paperback) | ISBN 9781499444155 (ebook)
Subjects: LCSH: Roosevelt, Theodore, 1858-1919–Miscellanea–Juvenile literature. | Presidents–United States–Biography–Miscellanea–Juvenile literature.
Classification: LCC E757 .K636 2024 (print) | LCC E757 (ebook) | DDC 973.91/1092 [B]–dc23/eng/20230810
LC record available at https://lccn.loc.gov/2023036954
LC ebook record available at https://lccn.loc.gov/2023036955

Manufactured in the United States of America

CONTENTS

EARLY LIFE

Many people think of Theodore Roosevelt as a wild outdoorsman who fought in wars, explored uncharted territory, climbed mountains, and enjoyed boxing. Would it surprise you to learn that Roosevelt was sickly and frail, or weak, as a child? It's true!

Theodore "Teddy" Roosevelt was born October 27, 1858. He was a frail boy, and he was often sick. When he was just three years old, Roosevelt began suffering from sudden **asthma** attacks. His parents, Theodore Sr. and Martha, feared he wouldn't survive.

IT'S A FACT!

WHEN ROOSEVELT WAS ALMOST A TEENAGER, HIS FATHER—A WEALTHY BUSINESSMAN AND **PHILANTHROPIST**—CHALLENGED HIS SON TO IMPROVE HIMSELF WITH EXERCISE, GYMNASTICS, AND BOXING. IT WORKED!

THEODORE ROOSEVELT SR.

THEODORE ROOSEVELT JR.

ROOSEVELT ONCE WROTE, "I WAS A SICKLY, DELICATE BOY, SUFFERED MUCH FROM CHRONIC [ONGOING] ASTHMA, AND FREQUENTLY HAD TO BE TAKEN AWAY ON TRIPS TO FIND A PLACE WHERE I COULD BREATHE."

MYTH OR FACT?

IN 1865, A SIX-YEAR-OLD TEDDY ROOSEVELT WATCHED FROM A SECOND-STORY WINDOW AS PRESIDENT ABRAHAM LINCOLN'S FUNERAL PROCESSION PASSED THROUGH NEW YORK CITY—AND THERE'S A PHOTOGRAPH TO PROVE IT!

FACT

After his **assassination** in 1865, Abraham Lincoln's funeral procession passed through numerous towns and cities on its way to Springfield, Illinois. The procession passed through New York City on April 24 of that year.

In the photo shown here, two figures can be seen in the window of the building on the left. This building, located at 849 Broadway, belonged to the Roosevelt family at the time. Several witnesses have said that the figures in the window are Teddy and his brother, Elliott.

THE BUILDING ON BROADWAY BELONGED TO CORNELIUS VAN SCHAACK ROOSEVELT, TEDDY AND ELLIOTT'S GRANDFATHER.

CONSERVATIONIST AND OUTDOORSMAN

MYTH OR FACT?

ROOSEVELT ESTABLISHED THE FIRST CONSERVATION ORGANIZATION IN NORTH AMERICA.

FACT

IN 1903, WHILE SERVING HIS FIRST TERM AS PRESIDENT, ROOSEVELT WENT ON A THREE-DAY CAMPING TRIP WITH NATURALIST JOHN MUIR. MUIR LED THEM THROUGH YOSEMITE NATIONAL PARK, WHERE THEY CAMPED AMONG GIANT SEQUOIA TREES.

From early in his life, Roosevelt was inspired by nature. Before he was even a teenager, he had collected hundreds of birds and animal **specimens**, a collection he called the "Roosevelt Museum of Natural History."

In 1887, Theodore Roosevelt and his friend George Bird Grinnell cofounded the Boone and Crockett Club. This was one of the first conservation organizations in the world! It helped to regulate, or control, hunting and fishing in the United States. It also helped establish national forests and national parks. This club still exists today.

IT'S A FACT!

ROOSEVELT'S POLICIES AS PRESIDENT ESTABLISHED ABOUT 230 MILLION ACRES (93.1 MILLION HA) OF PROTECTED PUBLIC LAND. HE ALSO BEGAN EFFORTS TO ESTABLISH THE NATIONAL PARK SERVICE.

BECOMING PRESIDENT

MYTH OR FACT?

ROOSEVELT WAS ELECTED PRESIDENT TWICE.

MYTH

From March to September 1901, Roosevelt served as vice president to President William McKinley. He unexpectedly became the country's 26th president when President McKinley was assassinated in Buffalo, New York. This made Roosevelt, at age 42, the youngest person to hold that office. Roosevelt served his first term without a vice president.

After finishing his first term, Roosevelt was elected in 1904 to the position of president of the United States. His vice president was Indiana senator Charles W. Fairbanks.

ROOSEVELT WAS SWORN INTO OFFICE IN THE HOME OF LAWYER ANSLEY WILCOX IN BUFFALO ON SEPTEMBER 14, 1901. TODAY, THE BUILDING IS KNOWN AS THE THEODORE ROOSEVELT **INAUGURAL** NATIONAL HISTORIC SITE.

MYTH OR FACT?

ROOSEVELT WAS THE FIRST PRESIDENT TO INVITE AN AFRICAN AMERICAN MAN TO DINE WITH HIM AT THE WHITE HOUSE.

FACT

In 1901, shortly after becoming the president, Roosevelt did something that many people considered shocking at the time. He invited African American educator Booker T. Washington to dine with him at the White House. This had never happened before! People were particularly angry that Roosevelt's wife and daughter were at the dinner.

Washington was a notable educator and a founder of the Tuskegee Institute in Alabama. Roosevelt wanted his opinion on the South, southern voters, and winning the Black vote.

IT'S A FACT!

IN 2008, AFTER LOSING THE PRESIDENTIAL ELECTION TO BARACK OBAMA, JOHN MCCAIN REFERRED TO THE DINNER BETWEEN ROOSEVELT AND WASHINGTON AS A TURNING POINT IN RACIAL RELATIONS IN THE UNITED STATES—A COUNTRY THAT HAD JUST ELECTED ITS FIRST BLACK PRESIDENT.

ROOSEVELT WAS HARSHLY **CRITICIZED** BY NEWSPAPERS AFTER THE NOW-FAMOUS DINNER. WASHINGTON, HOWEVER, RECEIVED DEATH THREATS FOR YEARS FOLLOWING THE EVENT.

THE SPORTING PRESIDENT

MYTH OR FACT?

PRESIDENT ROOSEVELT HATED THE SPORT OF AMERICAN FOOTBALL.

MYTH

American football was a hugely popular college sport in the late 1800s and early 1900s. However, it was also deadly. Players didn't wear a lot of padding or helmets. Ball carriers were often gang tackled and left bloodied and **injured**. The *Chicago Tribune* reported that, in 1904, there were 159 serious football injuries and 18 deaths.

Roosevelt was a fan of so-called "manly" sports, including American football. He felt it was a training ground for soldiers. However, he recognized the need to reform the sport he loved. In 1905, he invited representatives from major colleges to the White House to talk about changes.

THIS POLITICAL CARTOON FROM 1908 SHOWS WHAT MANY AMERICANS THOUGHT ABOUT THE SPORT OF FOOTBALL.

MYTH OR FACT?

ROOSEVELT LOST SIGHT IN ONE EYE DURING A BOXING MATCH AT THE WHITE HOUSE.

FACT

Roosevelt had bad eyesight his whole life. It kept him from playing some sports, but it didn't stop him from leading an active life, which included boxing. He was in the Harvard boxing club and continued to box after college.

In 1901, Roosevelt put a boxing ring in the White House basement. He regularly hosted boxing matches and even took part in them! In 1905, during a match with his friend Colonel Daniel T. Moore, Roosevelt took a hard hit, causing him to lose sight in his left eye.

IT'S A FACT!

LETTERS FROM ROOSEVELT SHOW THAT HE ENJOYED TRAINING IN JUDO AND JUJITSU, TWO JAPANESE **MARTIAL ARTS**, WHILE IN THE WHITE HOUSE. HE CONSIDERED THESE ATHLETIC ARTS SUPERIOR TO ALL OTHERS.

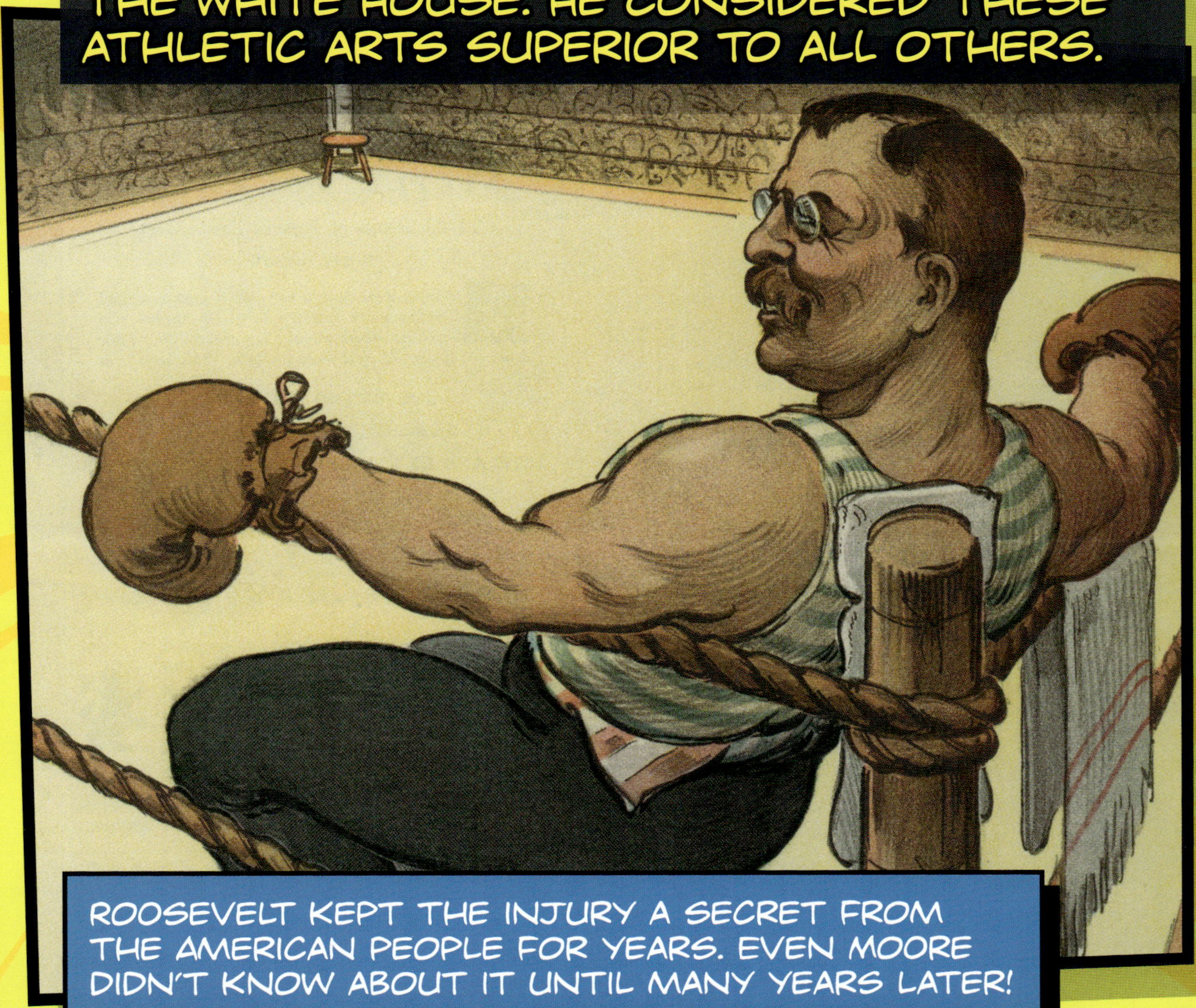

ROOSEVELT KEPT THE INJURY A SECRET FROM THE AMERICAN PEOPLE FOR YEARS. EVEN MOORE DIDN'T KNOW ABOUT IT UNTIL MANY YEARS LATER!

MYTH OR FACT?

ROOSEVELT ONCE RODE A BULL MOOSE—AND THERE'S A PHOTOGRAPH TO PROVE IT!

MYTH

Roosevelt's second term as president ended in 1909. He helped William Howard Taft win the election in 1908, but he wanted Taft to start creating more **progressive** policies. When Taft failed to do that, Roosevelt threw his hat into the ring one more time and ran for president under the newly formed progressive "Bull Moose Party."

The famous photo of Roosevelt riding a bull moose was part of a political advertisement for the 1912 presidential election. It also showed Republican Taft on an elephant and Democrat Woodrow Wilson on a donkey.

NEW-YORK TRIBUNE, SUNDAY, SEPTEMBER 8, 1912.

THE RACE FOR THE WHITE HOUSE.

Photos Copyright by Underwood & Underwood.

y Spent Among Men Who Were Atoning Sins Agai

THE IMAGE OF ROOSEVELT RIDING A BULL MOOSE WAS CREATED BY THE PHOTOGRAPHY COMPANY UNDERWOOD AND UNDERWOOD. THEY CUT ROOSEVELT OUT OF A PHOTOGRAPH OF HIM RIDING A HORSE AND ADDED IT TO A PHOTOGRAPH OF A BULL MOOSE.

THE BULL MOOSE

In 1912, while preparing to give a speech in Milwaukee, Wisconsin, Roosevelt was shot in the chest … but he still gave the speech! He began his speech by saying, "Ladies and gentlemen, I don't know whether you fully understand that I have just been shot, but it takes more than that to kill a bull moose." His speech was 90 minutes long. Only after he was done would he accept medical attention.

Roosevelt lost the election, but the Bull Moose Party received a higher percentage of votes than any other third party in U.S. history. Roosevelt was truly a living legend!

IT'S A FACT!

THE BULLET WAS SLOWED BY ROOSEVELT'S HEAVY OVERCOAT, HIS EYEGLASS CASE, AND HIS SPEECH, WHICH WERE ALL CRAMMED INTO THE INNER RIGHT JACKET POCKET. THE BULLET WAS NEVER REMOVED FROM HIS CHEST!

ROOSEVELT'S TIMELINE

OCTOBER 27, 1858	THEODORE "TEDDY" ROOSEVELT IS BORN IN NEW YORK CITY.
1876–1880	ROOSEVELT ATTENDS AND GRADUATES FROM HARVARD.
OCTOBER 27, 1880	HE MARRIES HIS FIRST WIFE, ALICE HATHAWAY LEE.
FEBRUARY 14, 1884	ROOSEVELT'S MOTHER AND WIFE BOTH DIE ON THE SAME DAY.
DECEMBER 2, 1886	ROOSEVELT MARRIES HIS CHILDHOOD SWEETHEART, EDITH CAROW.
1887	HE COFOUNDS THE BOONE AND CROCKETT CLUB.
1898	ROOSEVELT IS ELECTED GOVERNOR OF NEW YORK STATE.
1900	HE IS ELECTED VICE PRESIDENT.
SEPTEMBER 14, 1901	ROOSEVELT BECOMES THE 26TH PRESIDENT OF THE UNITED STATES.
1904	HE IS REELECTED PRESIDENT.
OCTOBER 14, 1912	ROOSEVELT IS SHOT IN THE CHEST BEFORE A SPEECH. HE STILL DELIVERS THE SPEECH.
JANUARY 16, 1919	ROOSEVELT DIES AT AGE 60.

GLOSSARY

assassination: The act of killing someone, especially a public figure.

asthma: A condition that makes it hard for a person to breathe.

conservation: Efforts to take care of the natural world.

criticize: To point out the faults of someone or something.

funeral procession: A group of vehicles or people traveling to or from a funeral.

inaugural: Having to do with a ceremonial induction into political office.

injure: To cause pain or harm to.

martial art: Any of several arts of combat and self-defense (such as karate and jujitsu) that are widely practiced as a sport.

philanthropist: A wealthy person who gives their money and time to help make life better for other people.

progressive: A person believing in gradual political change and social improvement by government action.

specimen: A part or a single thing (such as a bug or animal) that shows what the whole group is like.

FOR MORE INFORMATION

BOOKS

Harrison, Wag. *The Presidents Did What?* Richmond, VA: Belle Isle Books, 2021.

Huddleston, Emma. *Theodore Roosevelt*. Minneapolis, MN: North Star Editions, 2023.

Pettiford, Rebecca. *Theodore Roosevelt*. Minnetonka, MN: Bellwether Media, 2022.

WEBSITES

Biography: President Theodore Roosevelt
www.ducksters.com/biography/uspresidents/theodoreroosevelt.php
Learn much more about the life and presidency of Roosevelt here.

Theodore Roosevelt
www.biography.com/political-figures/theodore-roosevelt
Read more details about Roosevelt's life here.

INDEX